The Mastermind Groups can do miracles for you and your business. You can overcome your limits and improve both professionally and personally. Let the journey begin!

THE POWER OF
MASTERMIND
GROUP

The Secret Weapon
for your personal and professional Life

EDOARDO
ZELONI MAGELLI

Copyright © 2017 Edoardo Zeloni Magelli

All rights reserved

ISBN: 978-1-80120-476-7

First English Edition: November 2017

Original Edition: September 2017

"Il Potere del Mastermind Group: L'Arma Segreta per la tua Vita personale e professionale"

Author: Psychologist, Businessman and Consultant. Edoardo Zeloni Magelli, born in Prato in 1984. In 2010, soon after graduating in Psychology of Work and Organizations, he launched his first startup. As a Businessman he is CEO of Zeloni Corporation, a training company specialising in Business Applied Mental Sciences. His company is a reference point for anyone who wants to realize an idea or a project. As a scientist of the mind he is the father of Primordial Psychology and helps people to empower their minds in the shortest possible time. A music and sport-lover.

UPGRADE YOUR MIND → zelonimagelli.com

UPGRADE YOUR BUSINESS → zeloni.eu

The reproductions made for professional, economic or commercial purposes or otherwise for purposes other than personal use may only be made following a specific authorization issued by the author.

By reading this document, the reader agrees that under no circumstances is the author responsible for any losses, direct or indirect, which are incurred as a result of the use of information contained within this document, including, but not limited to, — errors, omissions, or inaccuracies.

CONTENTS

1.	**THE MASTERMIND GROUP**	7
2.	**THE HISTORY OF MASTERMIND**	13
3.	**THE SELECTION OF MEMBERS**	19
4.	**HOW IT WORKS**	27
5.	**THE ADVANTAGES OF THE MASTERMIND GROUP**	39
6.	**THE ROUND TABLE**	41
7.	**THE PEER GROUP**	45
8.	**FIND AND CREATE A GROUP**	49
9.	**SUGGESTIONS**	51
10	**SIMPOCEAN**	55

1

THE POWER OF MASTERMIND GROUP

The Mastermind Group is a very strong and powerful secret weapon that will soon become your way to success. It is an alliance of brains, a small peer group, who regularly meet in a spirit of harmony, to discuss and help each other to improve their own results.

The members of the group exchange ideas, information, advice, strategies and resources in order to help solve problems, overcome obstacles and overcome the challenges of their projects by using everybody's capabilities and ideas. It's an appointment to exchange views and improve their business. It is an opportunity to exchange ideas with other people of the same level but with different skills and experiences. It is a group that also becomes a strong personal and emotional support.

There are no hierarchies and all members are on the same level. Decisions are taken in a totally democratic way.

It is therefore an exchange between highly experienced people in certain fields who decide to share their experiences and skills to give and receive free training, and in addition have the desire to make their business grow, they also have the desire to help other members of the group without expecting an economic return.

From the Mastermind Group you can obtain a mixture of experience, training, knowledge, and it's a great opportunity to take advantage of the talents and capabilities of all the participants. Believe me, sometimes all you need is a simple idea or an expedient to revolutionize your life and your business. It's an opportunity to team up with other businessmen. Partnerships and joint ventures are often made, and even good friendships, even though this is not the primary objective, but, as often happens in a Mastermind group you become friends who help each other in business.

It's an appointment that is attended by people who have the same desire for personal and professional growth.

It is not an informal meeting, but should not be compared to an evening out with friends where you talk about general things, and take time away from the other members of the group who need advice.

Thanks to the Mastermind Group, one can also understand the processes that lead to success, the steps to be taken to achieve a goal, the strategies to be implemented to achieve results. It's an alliance of minds that makes you feel that you have achieved new skills as soon as you finish the meeting.

A group with these characteristics that moves towards a precise goal can dramatically multiply the successes of the group's components.

The Mastermind Group therefore becomes an opportunity to meet and discuss one or more topics that turns into a moment of mutual inspiration as often happened in ancient times.

"The Mastermind principle consists of an alliance of two or more minds working in perfect harmony for the attainment of a common definite objective. Success does not come without the cooperation of others"
Napoleon Hill

2

THE HYSTORY OF MASTERMIND

Over time humanity has forgotten that conversation is a true art. The past has been forgotten, the "past" that offered an invaluable set of tools to understand the present and to build the future.

The Human being is the same and the life of humanity is a continuous series of historical courses and recourses.

In ancient Greece and ancient Rome, the symposium (or convivium) was the convivial practice that followed a banquet, during which the participants ate, drank, talked, sang, played, danced and joked together.

The first written testimony of the symposium is on the so-called *Nestor Cup*, a geometric cup *(skyphos)*, of the second half of the 8th century B.C.

The word "Symposium" comes from Greek and means *drinking together*; convivium comes from Latin and means *living together*. There were two types: the *good symposium*, like the spartan *syssitia*, admired by many authors, and had become an example to be followed and praised of the sobriety of custom, where the participants shared food and drinks prescribed by law.

These meals were an educational means in which young people participated and witnessed political discussions; and the *bad symposium*, based on vulgarity, sexual excesses, and drinking wine in order to get drunk.

These were occasions for drinking and "love", during which the participants drank too much and gave free venting without limits to conversations as well as being occasions of political celebration and conspiracies. In the symposium, the participants had ideologies and aspirations of equal intent and recognized themselves as a political association formed by adult male citizens *(eteria),* and shared the same concept of life, usually inclined towards oligarchy. It was a moment of particularly important and articulated social life. It was a convention, a moment of cultural dialogue, a sort of collective ritual of exchange of ideas and opinions on various subjects, it combined the pleasure of conversing and of being together to poetry, music, dance, food and wine.

Sharing the meal had a social identification value and brought the people who participated closer to each other, the closeness was also due to the modest size of the banquet halls which allowed each of the diners to see and hear all the others.

Among the favorite topics of conversation, there were often philosophical and literary themes, and it was a moment of great political and social implications, but also ethical, sacred, and religious.

It was a training ground of wisdom made of sharp and cultured conversations.

The banquet was a true institution for the Greek aristocracy and for the ruling class who met to talk about politics and culture. With the passing of time, with the decrease of political conflicts and the development of city structures, the symposium became a private meeting among friends, while still maintaining the spirit of social aggregation.

Today, the concept is basically the same. The concept of the Mastermind Group (Mastermind Alliance) is treated, for the first time, with conviction, passion and enthusiasm by Napoleon Hill in his book *The Low of Success* published in 1920.

Hill was one of the first producers of the modern literary genre of personal success and was a consultant of the US President Franklin Roosevelt. He discovered that the secret of the people who had accumulated great wealth was in fact the presence of a support group.

He was inspired by the businessman Andrew Carnegie, a representative of the American dream. He left Scotland, where he was born, when he was very young in order to go to the United States to find fortune.

In 1865 he founded his company, the *Carnegie Steel Company*, which made Pittsburgh the capital of the iron and steel industry of Carnegie one of the richest men in the world.

He built one of the most powerful and influential companies in American history, and become very wealthy, according to some, his patrimony revalued in dollars was the second highest ever and the fifth highest in relation to the US gross national product.

At the age of sixty-five he sold his company to the banker J.P. Morgan for 480 million dollars and dedicated the rest of his life to writing and philanthropic activities and he donated around 350 million dollars to finance, co-fund and establish universities, libraries and museums around the world.

Andrew Carnegie was surrounded by a group of fifty men with the objective of becoming the leader of the production and sales of steel. He stated that the merit of his entire fortune was to be attributed to the power and knowledge accumulated through this group.

Napoleon Hill also interviewed the six richest people in Boston at the time. Here too it came to light that their secret was the presence of this support group. They met when they had nothing, but thanks to mutual help, exchange of experience, knowledge and resources they became successful. And even after achieving success their Mastermind Groups continued so that they could keep improving.

After Napoleon's Hill publication of *Think and Grow Rich* in 1937, his most famous work, a concentration of philosophy for success, the concept of the Mastermind Group developed and evolved to become a key instrument for successful people.

3

THE SELECTION OF THE MEMBERS

The key to the Mastermind Group is in the selection of the people. The quality of the people will determine the quality of the ideas and thoughts. With the right people you can create a very powerful support system with a long-term vision.

The group does not have an actual leader, there is a shared leadership, a group of people who share similar values and have competences of the same level.

> *"Before you look at what you are eating and drinking, it is necessary to see who you are doing it with; in fact, eating without friends is a life of a wolf or a lion"*

This principle of Epicurus, quoted by Seneca in his nineteenth letter to Lucilius, highlights the importance of the choice of diners.

It was good advice for members of the high Roman society who could not risk sitting at a table with their *"clients"* (the *"Cliens"* was the citizen who had to fulfill a series of obligations towards a *"patronus"*) because they were acting out of opportunistic reasons and not through an honest friendship.

> *"Errat autem qui amicum in atrio quaerit, in convivio probat"*

"The one who searches for a friend in the entrance hall and then puts him to the test in the banquet makes a mistake"

Under certain conditions, everyone may seem to be a friend, but in order to find a true friend, we should think of the people who have been close to us and who have supported us in times of difficulty.

This is applicable to many different contexts that makes us realize that the people who become long lasting, true friends are not the people we meet in venues and parties, but those who we share our time, passions and projects with.

If you are the only one to give advice then you are in the wrong group.

One of the key points of the Mastermind Group is reciprocity.

- People who should never be part of your Mastermind Group are good people with good intentions but who have no skills and are not geared towards results. These people are not useful. These are the typical people who are clever with words, have many ideas, but who have never achieved anything, therefore they are not practical. They are also the ones who prefer going out for a drink rather than creating something, when it is time to work.

- You need motivated, positive people who are orientated towards abundance. You need to exchange ideas with people who want to develop excellent long-term relationships. Positive people with the right mindset, set to improve themselves and their projects.

- You need members with problem solving skills.

- You need people with a direct experience in what they do. The enthusiasts and the mediators who are passionate but who have never directly participated in activities are not the right people.

- There is not even room for egocentric and centralizing people who want all the benefits for themselves, that is, those who take without giving. They are people who continually take from others without giving value back. The Mastermind Group is based on the exchange of ideas and experiences.

- Even though the participants share the same interests, they must not be of the same field, they should not all have the same experience, they must not have the same skills, they should not all be of the same sex and age. These are all very important factors because diversity is necessary to learn from each other, to exchange ideas and thoughts that can enrich us, to see from different points of view, and different perspectives.

The diversification of the group is a very important element and is necessary to take advantage of what is, in my opinion, the most powerful existing weapon: *LEARNING TRANSFER.*

The learning Transfer is devastating, it can give you a competitive advantage that is not be easily accessible by most people.

The Learning Transfer is a learning technique that is based on learning from multiple fields to allow you to have new suggestions and ideas that you would never have achieved by studying in your own field alone.

It is a strategy that is put into practice when we acquire new knowledge in a field and we have the ability to apply it to other areas. Illumination and revolutions occur when we are able to apply notions learned from a different field, other than our own and we are able to establish new connections thanks to our critical thinking ability.

Studying information with this technique allows you to strengthen your brain muscles that allow you to establish new connections to make you see new horizons. You will learn to connect all the information of the various fields and take advantage of the immense power that this technique generates. Knowledge is devastating. We have so many things to learn and the more you study, the more you realize how much in fact you do not know.

Life must be a continuous study in order to improve our lives and widen our horizons, it is the protection against the illusion and the misconception of ourselves and the surrounding world.

Without doubt, we can draw from different knowledge and grow considerably by taking advantage of the power of the Mastermind Group.

After selecting the members, it is also useful to draw up an agreement between the participants. No one enters the group definitively until they attend for the second time. It is useful to allow new candidates to do a no-obligation trial. You agree to let a person try the Mastermind experience once or twice. After the second meeting, if everyone agrees, the new member can join the group. It is important that the people who join the Mastermind Group are able to provide added value to the other members, and if they do not fulfill the regulations and do not add any value after the first test, then their participation is cancelled.

In the Mastermind Group you need commitment, it is a long-term support system. Members must ensure their presence and engage in a regular and

punctual attendance. The ideal number of participants for a quality Mastermind Group is between 4 and 8 people. It is an optimal number that allows you to go deep into the discussion topics. In larger groups, there is risk of confusion and little time to dedicate to each of the participants. It is also useful to have a confidentiality agreement between the members. Meetings must be secret away from indiscrete eyes and whatever happens in the Mastermind Group remains in the Mastermind Group.

4

HOW IT WORKS

For a quality Mastermind Group, it is important to have an accurate planning. It is important to have rules and regulations to structure the meetings. First of all, you have to elect the conductor, mediator and facilitator, the *King of the Symposium*.

A role that can change from one session to another and that can be exchanged among the members.

The King of the Symposium was a guest who had the task of managing and animating the party.

He was elected with a crown of flowers or of ivy leaves which was more beautiful than the crowns of the other guests.

The conductor is fundamental to ensure that the timing is respected during the session.

The Mastermind is not a chat among friends, but a moment of insight, inspiration and motivation. You can meet physically or virtually by taking advantage of tools that allow you to overcome the limits of space and distances such as: *Skype, Zoom* or *Hangouts*.

The basis of the Mastermind Group is sharing all that is considered significant to you and to the other members.

You share objectives and problems, deal with topics, reflect on proposals received, on customer feedback, motivate each other, bring books to consult, recommend books to read, read quotes to reflect on and talk about the software to use.

During these meetings, we enhance ourselves by giving and receiving, exchanging experiences, suggestions and knowledge, and finally setting goals for the next session.

It is important to keep to the program without wandering off on other issues that are not related to the Mastermind. It's useful to leave your private life out of the Mastermind or if you want to talk about it you can do so at the end of the meeting.

LOCATION

It can take place anywhere, the important thing is that it is an environment that guarantees privacy and focus, an environment without distractions and interruptions. It can be organized to be held at someone's home, in a villa, in hotel rooms, farmhouses, spas, deserted beaches and sometimes even in restaurants, although it is not the ideal environment due to interruptions and lack of focus.

THE SCHEDULE

It is important to decide which topics you want to deal with and in which way. The best way to start a Mastermind is to share the goals and the small successes achieved from the previous session.

Members take turns in sharing their results making the others aware of them. This helps to set up the meeting.

For the first meetings it is useful to discuss general aspects of the topics before going into the specifics. It is suggested to always draw up a schedule and establish the topics you want to talk about, for example:

- The day of Productivity and Time Management

- The Marketing day

- The Sales day
- The Brainstorming day
- The Human Resources day
- The Client Management day
- The Research and Development day
- The Digital automation day
- The Future day

Then you deal with questions such as:

- What are the major difficulties you are encountering lately?

- How did you deal with and overcome that difficulty?

- What strategies did you use to achieve your results?

- What is the most important event that has happened to you since the last meeting?

- What are the new opportunities?

- What are the most important goals?

- What is the new challenge you want to overcome?

An example of the agenda could be:

- Celebration of successes

- Analysis of the goals of the previous session and any problems encountered

- Analysis of successful strategies that have achieved results

- Talk about the topic of the day or a theme you choose

- Analyze the participant's problems with respective ideas, tips and strategies to overcome them

- Establish the targets to review during the next meeting.

TIME E DURATION

There are many possibilities, and you are free to choose the time and duration that you prefer. You could organize your Mastermind with these intervals:

- Weekly meetings of the duration of approx. 90 mins

- A whole day once a month

- Two intensive days every season

- One week a year

It is important to respect the planned time and schedule, the risk is to turn the Mastermind Group into a meeting of friends, which, despite being pleasant, will not allow you to achieve goals of professional growth.

You take it in turns to answer questions while the others are completely silent and take notes, writing down ideas and solutions on how to help the others.

In order to maintain the group efficient, it is always good to have a timer to help manage timing. There are always long-winded people who talk too much.

The timer allows everyone to have the same amount of time to speak. You always talk with a timer, everyone has a certain number of minutes to comment and help overcome the challenges.

It may also happen that you have to announce an extraordinary session if one of the members of the group is experiencing an emergency situation.

THE HOT SEAT

One of the best ways to carry out a Mastermind is to use the Hot Seat technique. Sitting on the Hot Seat means that you have the opportunity to talk about your difficulties and ask for help.

It's the seat where a member and his business are in the spotlight, at the center of the meeting, all the attention is on them. It is the most selfish and unselfish situation of all. When it is our turn, we must prepare ourselves to be selfish in the sense of making the best use of this experience to get the most support, so that we can grow and improve.

It's being selfish in order to be more altruistic. You will get the most out of the others under the spotlight. You sit down and keep to the agenda and ask for what you need. It's the right moment to get all the help and support you can from the group. When it is your turn, you must be eager for knowledge and to ask for help. If you do it you will raise the level of your activities.

Victories are shared and feedback is received on what is being done. This leaves you under pressure until the next session and will push you to do better and achieve more results because then you will go back into the spotlight to talk about yourself. This will make you become more responsible.

- What are you working at?

- How did you reach those results?

- What isn't working?

- What sort of help do you need?

You should never feel under examination the group is your ally. When your time comes to talk, even if you haven't achieved evident results, try to find a small success. Such as having new subscribers to the newsletter, having increased visits to the website or having received compliments from someone. Even though these are small successes they must be shared with the group.

5

THE ADVANTAGES OF THE MASTERMIND GROUP

Taking part in a Mastermind Group accelerates your transformation, improves your personal vision and your business, and offers you many benefits, in summary:

- Reciprocal support

- Exchange and access to different resources, know-how and strategies

- Different points of view and new perspectives

- Network creation and expansion

- Profound relationships

- Personal responsibility and inspiration

- Sharing

- Managing to focalize and remain concentrated on the goals

6

THE ROUND TABLE

Occasionally it may happen that you have to arrange a Round Table. The Round Table was the table of Camelot's Castle where King Arthur and his Knights sat to discuss matters of crucial importance to the kingdom. The purpose of the Round Table was to avoid prestige conflicts.

In fact, since there was no head of the table, every knight, including the King, had an equal place with all the others, and King Arthur felt just like every other knight.

The Round Table today is a situation of further

confrontation. It is a meeting-event with a small number of specialized participants and open to the public. The purpose of a round table is to talk about a theme of recent affairs.

An event where there is a continuous interaction between the participants and the audience. The participants will have to come to the debate prepared on the topics that will be dealt with. You start by going through a checklist of things to do for the success of the event.

You decide the theme and the title of the Round Table, then after inspection you choose the location, study the placements, think about the collaborators and study the timing.

The next step is to contact the people who are invited, make an estimate of the probable participants.

You send the invitations, either in paper form or digitally, and you check the acoustics of the chosen location.

It is also a good idea to contact a catering company to arrange a banquet for those who are attending, this is always appreciated.

The communication of the event is very important. Both invitations and all advertising material must state the title of the Round Table, you must understand the topics discussed, it must be clear who the promoters are, who the speakers are and of course the date, time, city and address of the location and the room number.

It is also useful to provide a map to get to the location also indicating the transport you can take. Furthermore, the participation fee and the enrollment method must be clear.

Promotion will be fundamental. It will need to be advertised taking advantage of the potential of the web, therefore, the website, mail marketing, social networks and above all through our funnel. You can also take advantage of traditional advertising such as billboards, mobile billboard trucks and flyer distribution at the city's strategic points.

If there are any participants coming from abroad, it is necessary to arrange for their stay by identifying the appropriate accommodation facilities, taking into account the quality of their services and the proximity to the location.

7

THE PEER GROUP

"You are the average of the 5 people you spend the most time with" Jim Rohn

The people that surround us have a certain influence on us. To know how much a person earns, identify their five closest friends and calculate their average income.

To understand the aspirations of a person, identify his five dearest friends and you will find the answer. If you want to understand and evaluate a person, identify his five best friends and you will have an idea.

When you are self-employed, you also often face personal loneliness. People do not understand your choices, others make fun of them, others ignore them altogether.

You cannot continue to listen to those who do not believe in your qualities and abilities. If you frequent an environment that you don't trust, you end up with the risk of persuading yourself that you have little faith in yourself and that you are not capable.

> *"Let go of negative people, they only show up to share complaints, problems, disastrous stories, fear, and judgment on others. If somebody is looking for a bin to throw all their trash into, make sure it's not in your mind."* Dalai Lama

The vision of the world of people that we spend time with has a great impact on us. Human beings are social animals who tends to mix with other individuals and establish themselves in societies. The relationships that we have influence our personal stories and beliefs.

We should never blame others for the course of our lives, but the people we frequent affect our perception of reality. We can choose the people we share our time with. Those to spend our days and share our passions with. We must surround ourselves with people who vibrate on the same frequencies as ours.

You need to surround yourself with people who help you grow, people who share the same vision as you, allies that support you, people who encourage you and motivate you. Stay away from people who are against your ideas and projects.

You must look for people who have already obtained results and success in that area, ask them to tell you about their experiences, and teach you their strategies. Only those who have obtained results in an industry can teach you how to achieve those results in that field. You have to always be inspired by successful people. Your added value will be to surround yourself with fully established people. You must be a sponge and absorb everything that surrounds you in order to grow.

"If you are the most intelligent person in the room, you're in the wrong room"

8

FIND AND CREATE A GROUP

In order to find or create a group, you must, first of all, have a basic requirement: Motivation. If you are motivated you can start finding people interested in starting this activity. Creating a Mastermind is easy if you find the right people. Start with contacting a trusted person at the same level who wants advice and wants to grow his business, then you can think about the other members.

If they do not know what you're talking about, you can give them this book. Identify your skill niche and before you start talking to others about certain topics, start studying them and be prepared.

To find your future participants in the Mastermind, you can take advantage of the social network service *Meetup*, a platform designed to make meeting other people from all over the world, easy, forming groups created around a common interest.

You must be willing to invest your time to put the advice and the elements that Mastermind gives you into action. It is otherwise useless to participate. Remember to always put into practice the strategies and tips you receive. It is not enough to know. Without putting them into practice it is useless to participate in a Mastermind Group. Also, remember that in life, it is not sufficient to have ideas. Putting the ideas into practice is what makes the difference.

9

SUGGESTIONS

In my meetings, a few days before we meet, I usually send the agenda and the schedule with the points to be discussed to the members of the group, this helps everyone to be more prepared, focused and aware at the meeting.

It's a strategy that also gives another benefit. As soon as they finish reading the program, their brains will unconsciously start thinking about ideas and solutions right up to the day of the meeting.

And believe me, the best ideas often come when you're busy doing other things. It often happens that you get to the meeting with problems that are already solved and new ideas.

This makes us more effective and efficient.

There must always be someone who writes a detailed report on all the topics discussed and then passes it on to all the participants.

Another recommendation, dedicated to improving concentration, is to change places often, never sit in the same place, and change positions during the same session.

This variation of continuous stimulus allows you to keep the concentration level high and stimulates new points of view and perspectives.

Many of my colleagues, students and clients who apply my *Continuous Stimulation Variation* (*Zeloni Magelli's Continuous Stimulation Variation*) obtain a remarkable increase in daily productivity and keep up the concentration.

A diktat (a non-negotiable imposed condition) that we run into our Mastermind Group is total disconnection.

All phones must be turned off (this means off, not just on silent mode) no checking e-mails, no pcs or use of the internet. When Internet is needed for the research of more information or the use of the pc for any reason, this is done at end of the meeting. During the Mastermind Group total disconnection from others and from the outside world rules.

It is important that all participants declare their goals in front of everyone at the final stage of the meeting. Do not hold back, do not be scared to yell them out like when you shout in a changing room before a match. Declare your goals aloud, it will help you to be more concrete and it will make you work harder.

When you reach a goal or even a small achievement get into the habit of celebrating.

Maybe with a dinner, a bottle of champagne, no matter how but it's important that you do it. It is a very powerful anchorage tool that will remain a witness to the results achieved at that time. Celebrate your achievements, even the small ones, at the first opportunity.

Another suggestion I feel like giving to you is to have more Mastermind Groups for each area of your life. Each with different times and durations. In some groups ninety minutes per week are enough, in others the monthly frequency is the best, and in others the annual frequency works. It will be up to you to understand what the best situation is to make your group better.

10

SIMPOCEAN

I wonder if you are curious to know that before we can talk about the Simpocean we must talk about Atlantis, the ancient underwater and missing island in the night of time.

It is described for the first time in Plato's *Timeo* dialogue around 355 BC, one of the most important and influential writings in which Plato examines the nature and origin of the universe and of human nature. It is thanks to Plato's writings that humanity has come to know about Atlantis.

[…] This power came forth out of the Atlantic Ocean, for in those days the Atlantic was navigable; and there was an island situated in front of the straits which are by you called the Pillars of Heracles; the island was larger than Libya and Asia put together, and was the way to other islands, and from these you might pass to the whole of the opposite continent which surrounded the true ocean; for this sea which is within the Straits of Heracles is only a harbor, having a narrow entrance, but that other is a real sea, and the surrounding land may be most truly called a boundless continent. Now in this island of Atlantis there was a great and wonderful empire which had rule over the whole island and several others, and over parts of the continent, and, furthermore, the men of Atlantis had subjected the parts of Libya within the columns of Heracles as far as Egypt, and of Europe as far as Tyrrhenia. […]

Before the greatest civilizations were born, there was an extremely evolved and technologically advanced population, the inhabitants of Atlantis. Atlantis was a country inhabited by perfection, its civilization reached its fullest splendor around 9000 BC and brought culture and civilization to the world.

It was paradise on earth. It was rich in precious minerals, fertile soils, forests and wildlife, the land generated abundant goods and produce. There were temples, royal palaces, harbors, and other majestic works. It had become a powerful kingdom in the midst of the Atlantic with its mountains in the north and along the coast, down to the southern plains.

The island was divided into ten areas, and the ten sons of Poseidon became their kings. It was governed by the sons of the God of the sea. Around 9600 BC most of Western Europe and Africa were conquered by the Atlantis Empire.

This date coincides with the end of the last ice age

and the birth of the first city-states, discovered in present-day Iraq. After having tried to conquer Athens, Atlantis which had become corrupt, a condition that had ruined a peaceful, wealthy and extremely wise society, was destroyed and drowned with terrible cataclysms by Poseidon.

[...] But afterwards there occurred violent earthquakes and floods; and in a single day and night of misfortune all your warlike men in a body sank into the earth, and the island of Atlantis in like manner disappeared in the depths of the sea. [...]

Ignatius Donnelly, a politician, essayist, and American researcher, author of the book *The Antediluvian World* published in 1882, believed that many of the technologies used to develop metallurgy, agriculture and construction, and other conquests of humanity such as religion and language, had origins in Atlantis, which then spread knowledge to ancient populations who did not have such skills.

It is a theory similar to the **Theory of Paleocontact** or *Paleoastronautic Theory,* the group of theories that hypothesize a contact between extraterrestrial civilizations that intervened on the knowledge of ancient evolved human civilizations such as the Sumerians, the Egyptians, the civilizations of ancient India and the pre-Columbian.

Macaronesia. A collective name to indicate the various archipelagos of the North Atlantic Ocean located off the coast of Africa. A geographical position that coincides with Plat's description, beyond the Pillars of Hercules, just outside the Strait of Gibraltar.

The islands of Macaronesia are considered what remain of the ancient and lost continent. Macaronesia derives from the Greek μακάρων νῆσοι (makaròn nêsoi) and means *Islands of the Blessed*, an expression used by ancient Greek geographers to refer to some islands that were beyond the Strait of Gibraltar.

They are the *Lucky Islands* where the Gods welcomed heroes and mortals of extraordinary nature.

And it is just outside the Hercules Pillars, where the **SIMPOCEAN** takes place - **The Annual Summit of Mastermind Groups.** *The Mastermind Group of the highly evolved Mastermind Groups.*

The Symposium of the Islands of the Blessed.

It is located on the Lucky Islands, on a volcanic island in the middle of the Atlantic nominated a biosphere reserve by UNESCO, in a terrestrial paradise such as Atlantis, on the first and most geologically ancient island of the Canary Islands, part of Macaronesia: the island of Fuerteventura.

A week of Mastermind in the Atlantic Ocean. An event where members of Mastermind Groups talk to other members of other Mastermind Groups to increase their knowledge exponentially in a disproportionate way with valuable benefits. It is an opportunity of precious exchange with world-class people who can help expand your business boundaries and strengthen your network globally.

The search for the Lost Continent Atlantis has lasted for thousands of years, like the search for truth and lost knowledge, Plato's writings are like a treasure map just like the strategies of the Simpocean Mastermind Group.

It is taking advantage of Poseidon's power to revoke skill tsunamis, cataclysms of knowledge and destruction and the collapse of ignorance.

The Simpocean welcomes heroes of knowledge and men of extraordinary will to rediscover the art of conversation and dialogue. From the Platonic dialogues one finds oneself conversing in the ancient convivium and symposium. We go back to cultivating knowledge like we do wheat.

It is a hymn to Knowledge, Culture, Wisdom, Art and Justice, to go back to being the evolved and technologically advanced population of Atlantis.

THE SELECTION

Only members of the *50 List* can take part in the Simpocean, a very powerful list, just like its number. You can become part of the list only after an accurate and careful selection.

The selection is open to people from all over the world and anyone can apply. The world is always in need of new brains, new ideas, clever and motivated people.

The selection of the Simpocean is a worldwide selection of brains. If you think you have a particular talent, you want to grow, and you want to build something important, then you should apply for the selection. The selection of candidates takes part in a real Mastermind Group. During which skills, abilities, achievements, quality of ideas, and all of the fundamental requirements will be evaluated in order to become part of an evolved Mastermind group.

All candidates will be given a score and will become part of a global classification and sub-classifications divided into categories.

To participate in the selection, all you need to do is take part in at least one of the accredited mastermind events that you will find on the official Summit website: **simpocean.net**

If you are a mastermind event organiser you can apply to have your event accredited as well, simply go to the website and send your mastermind program for evaluation. If successful, your event will be accredited.

HOW THE SIMPOCEAN FUNCTIONS

The week on the island of Fuerteventura takes place in complete secrecy and away from indiscrete eyes. The week is divided into:

- **DAY 1**: Mental Regeneration: Meditation, Mindfulness and other activities.

- **DAY 2-3:** The members of the *50 List* are put into smaller groups and this is the beginning of several separate meetings. Thanks to the advanced technique of the *Group Dynamics of Cross Crossing by Zeloni Magelli* we will take advantage of the benefit of a Mastermind Group of 4-8 participants, and a proper exchange of knowledge among all the members will be encouraged.

- **DAY 4:** Global meeting.

- **DAY 5:** Tour of the Island.

- **DAY 6:** The day of visions and the creation of new networks.

- **DAY 7:** Free day to let your imagination run wild.

MASTERMIND EVENTS

Here you will find a list of some accredited and open to the public mastermind events where you too can participate.

There is no magic wand to be successful, but there are shortcuts. Getting the right information right away will help you avoid a long and tortuous path of trial and error. This will save you time, money, energy and resources because you will immediately learn about what works and what doesn't.

MIND MASTERMIND: The 1st Mastermind in the World on Empowered Mind where you can increase the power of your Mind.

THE MASTERMIND WEEKEND: The Marketing, Sales and Corporate Financial Management Training Weekend specialising in Business Applied Mental Sciences. A weekend to learn the best international best practices and to be able to compare with other entrepreneurs and self-employed in the middle of the Tuscan hills.

HYBRID MASTERMIND: Gain 100 years of experience in just 7 days by harnessing the power of the mastermind. It is the event that has given birth to a new generation of hybrid experiences: Training, Nature and Sustainable Tourism.

THE NEW YEAR'S CENHOLDING: The CenHolding is "The Great Mastermind Dinner" on December 29th - also jokingly called as the dinner that gives you a two-day lead over your competitors - where new startups find private financing and investors and business angels find new investment opportunities.

Over time it has become a true epicentre of international investment. Surely it is the dinner to start the New Year right and be sure to be in the middle of the flow of information that matters. Sometimes one dinner is enough to revolutionize your life and your business!

DIAMENE MASTERMIND INNER CIRCLE: This is my Inner Circle where I work with only 8 people a year. If that's you, I'll personally work with you, along with 7 other extraordinary people, to empower your mind and your business to help you perform better in every area and double your profits in the next 12 months.

This may seem like a bold and ambitious premise to you, but it's based on totally undeniable results that my clients and I have been achieving since 2010. This is thanks to well-tested techniques, strategies and methods that work great and that every year become more and more refined, thanks to the direct experience and knowledge that I continue to acquire during the mastermind in which I take part.

"Lucky is the person who will learn to master the Power of Mastermind"

Dr. Edoardo Zeloni Magelli

Imagine starting to read a book a week and creating a Mastermind Group with 7 other people reading a book a week.

Imagine exchanging your knowledge with that of others to get to know the 20% that guarantees you 80% of the results.

Can you understand the extraordinary personal and professional growth you could have with a Mastermind Group?

Thanks to this book you have come to know a great power. Now it is up to you.

Think big. Widen your horizons. When you are surrounded by incredible people, you can do incredible things.

"An investment in knowledge always pays the best interest"

Benjamin Franklin

UPGRADE YOUR MIND → zelonimagelli.com

UPGRADE YOUR BUSINESS → zeloni.eu

Edoardo Zeloni Magelli
Atlantide
Settembre 2017

www.ingramcontent.com/pod-product-compliance
Lightning Source LLC
Chambersburg PA
CBHW072208100526
44589CB00015B/2429